NATIONAL
GEOGRAPHIC

CHINESE
CIVILIZATION

PICTURE CREDITS
Cover, pages 16–17, 25 Image Bank/Getty Images; page 1 Victor R. Boswell Jr.; pages 3 top, 6 Christie's Images/Corbis; pages 3 center top, 10 Musee des Beaux-Arts, Orleans, France/Bridgeman Art Library; pages 3 center bottom, 34–35 Stone/Getty Images; page 3 bottom Arthur M. Sackler Museum, Harvard University Art Museums/Bridgeman Art Library; pages 4–5 Dean Conger; page 8 Asian Art and Architecture, Inc./Corbis; page 9 top Bradley Mayhew/Lonely Planet Images; pages 9 middle, 61 Biblioteque Nationale, Paris, France/Bridgeman Art Library; pages 9 bottom, 62 top Roy Parkes, Eye Ubiquitous/Corbis; page 12 The Travelsite/Picture Desk; page 14 British Museum, London, UK/Bridgeman Art Library; page 15 Walter Hodges/Corbis; pages 19, 62 bottom Private Collection/Bridgeman Art Library; page 20 Chinapix; pages 21, 50–51 Taxi/Getty Images; pages 22, 28, 40–41 Art Archive; page 23 The Barnes Foundation, Merion, Pennsylvania, USA/Bridgeman Art Library; page 24 Giraudon/Art Resource, NY; page 26 Hsien-min Yang; pages 27, 32, 33 left, 33 top, 57 top, 58 O. Louis Mazzatenta/National Geographic Image Collection; page 29 Yang Li Min/H.K. China Tourism Press; page 30 Robert Harding Images/Getty Images; page 31 Hongnian Zhang; page 33 right Doug Stern; page 36 Michael Yamashita; page 37 Frank Carter/Lonely Planet Images; pages 38–39 Michael Yamashita/National Geographic Image Collection; page 41 Institut des Hautes Etudes Chinoises, Paris/Bridgeman Art Library; page 43 Peter Guttman/Corbis; pages 44–45 top Museum of Fine Arts, Boston, Massachusetts, USA/Bridgeman Art Library; pages 44–45 bottom HIP/Scala/Art Resource, NY; pages 46 left and right, 47 left Keren Su; page 47 right Kevin R. Morris/Corbis; pages 48-49 National Geographic Maps; page 49 Fabian Cevallos/Corbis Sygma; page 52 Jacqui Hurst/Corbis; page 53 bottom Dean Conger/Corbis; page 53 top Michael Freeman/Corbis; page 54 right Liu Liqun/Corbis; page 54 center Keren Su/Corbis; page 54 left Ontario Science Center; page 55 Bridgeman Art Library/Getty Images; pages 56 top, 59 top, 64 Werner Forman/Art Resource, NY; page 56 bottom Seth Joel/Woodfin Camp & Associates; page 57 bottom Dennis Cox; page 59 bottom Courtesy of the Royal Ontario Toronto Museum, Toronto; page 60 Freelance Consulting Services Pty Ltd/Corbis.

Produced through the worldwide resources of the National Geographic Society, John M. Fahey, Jr., President and Chief Executive Officer; Gilbert M. Grosvenor, Chairman of the Board; Nina D. Hoffman, Executive Vice President and President, Books and Education Publishing Group.

PREPARED BY NATIONAL GEOGRAPHIC SCHOOL PUBLISHING
Ericka Markman, Senior Vice President and President Children's Books and Education Publishing Group; Steve Mico, Senior Vice President, Editorial Director; Marianne Hiland, Executive Editor; Richard Easby, Editorial Manager; Anita Schwartz, Project Editor; Jim Hiscott, Design Manager; Kristin Hanneman, Illustrations Manager; Matt Wascavage, Manager of Publishing Services; Sean Philpotts, Production Manager; Jane Ponton, Production Artist.

MANUFACTURING AND QUALITY MANAGEMENT
Christopher A. Liedel, Chief Financial Officer; Phillip L. Schlosser, Director; Clifton M. Brown III, Manager.

ART DIRECTION Dan Banks, Project Design Company

CONSULTANT/REVIEWER
Dr. Rhoads Murphey, Professor of History, University of Michigan

BOOK DEVELOPMENT Nieman Inc.

BOOK DESIGN Three Communication Design, LLC

PICTURE EDITING Paula McLeod, Worth a Thousand Words, Inc.

MAP DEVELOPMENT AND PRODUCTION Mapping Specialists, Ltd.

Copyright © 2005 National Geographic Society. All rights reserved. Reproduction of the whole or any part of the contents without written permission from the publisher is prohibited. National Geographic, National Geographic School Publishing, National Geographic Reading Expeditions, and the Yellow Border are registered trademarks of the National Geographic Society.

Published by the National Geographic Society
1145 17th Street, N.W.
Washington, D.C. 20036-4688

ISBN: 0-7922-4942-9

First Printing January, 2005
Printed in Canada

cover: Chinese fisherman using trained birds known as cormorants to catch fish **page 1:** Clay warrior from the tomb of Shi Huangdi, China's first emperor **page 3** (top): Figurine of a woman from the Tang dynasty **page 3** (center right): Calligrapher at work **page 3** (center left): The Great Wall of China **page 3** (bottom): Bronze vessel from the Shang dynasty

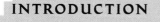

CHINESE
CIVILIZATION

China's last ruling family built their beautiful Summer Palace on the hills surrounding a lake near the capital, Beijing.

The ancient Chinese called their land the "Middle Kingdom." They saw it as the civilized center of the world, a realm of peace and order surrounded by wilderness where uncivilized peoples lived. Within natural barriers of mountains, deserts, and oceans, the Chinese developed their own distinctive way of life.

CIVILIZATION IN CHINA presents an unbroken line of development from its earliest appearance more than 3,500 years ago to the present day. This long tradition has given the Chinese a great respect for their past.

Chinese civilization first arose in northern China in the valley of the Huang He (hwahng huh), or "Yellow River." The river got its name from the yellow **silt**, or mud, that colors its waters. When the Huang He floods each year, it leaves behind a fertile layer of silt on the lowlands through which it flows, producing some of China's best farmland. More than 7,000 years ago, farming settlements began to develop there. By about 2000 B.C., these settlements had grown into China's first cities.

The history of China is divided into the periods in which different ruling families, or **dynasties,** were in power.

Figurine of a woman from the Tang dynasty

Length of Recorded History

3000 B.C. Writing invented in Near East

1600 B.C.
Rise of Shang dynasty

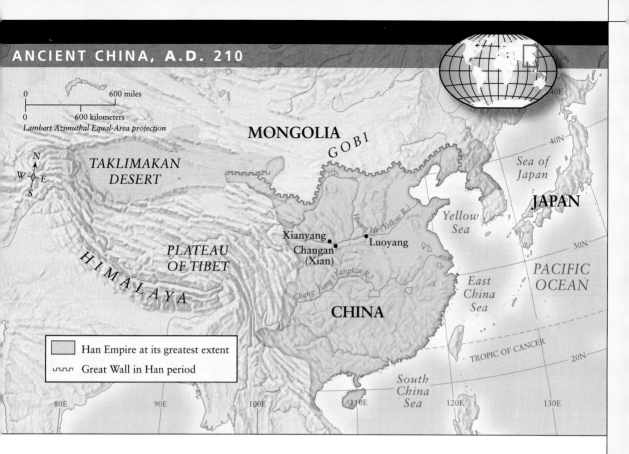

0 — 600 miles
0 — 600 kilometers
Lambert Azimuthal Equal-Area projection

MONGOLIA

GOBI

TAKLIMAKAN DESERT

Sea of Japan

JAPAN

40N

PLATEAU OF TIBET

HIMALAYA

Xianyang
Changan (Xian)
Luoyang

Huang He (Yellow R.)

Yellow Sea

30N

Yangtze R.

Chang Jiang

CHINA

East China Sea

PACIFIC OCEAN

20N

South China Sea

Han Empire at its greatest extent

Great Wall in Han period

TROPIC OF CANCER

80E   90E   100E   110E   120E   130E

The earliest Chinese dynasty for which historical records exist is the Shang, who came to power about 1600 B.C. During the Shang period, the ancient Chinese developed their system of writing.

About 500 years later, the Zhou (joh), a people from China's western borders, invaded northern China. They overthrew the Shang and established China's longest-lasting dynasty. The most important legacy of the Zhou period was the teachings of Confucius (kuhn–FYOO–shuhs). His ideas stressed the importance of tradition and the family. He has influenced China more than any other religious figure or social thinker in its history.

A.D. 1

A.D. 2000

A.D. 220
End of Han dynasty

Han dynasty oil lamp

Throughout China's history, one of the greatest challenges facing its rulers has been to unite the people of this vast region into a single society. There were long periods marked by warfare between rival kingdoms. Finally, two dynasties—the Qin (chin) and the Han—succeeded in unifying China under the strong rule of an emperor.

To govern their empire, China's rulers established the Chinese **civil service,** the large group of officials who ran the government. Throughout China's later history, this civil service had an important role in unifying Chinese society.

Under the Han, the influence of Chinese civilization began to be felt beyond China's borders. Chinese silk became one of the most valuable trade goods of the ancient world.

The Chinese of the Han Empire also produced inventions that would have great effects later, such as paper and the compass.

The articles in this book describe how Chinese civilization developed and influenced the rest of the world. To help guide your reading, they have been organized around the following three **BIG IDEAS:**

1 Chinese civilization is characterized by a great respect for the past.

2 The creation of a powerful Chinese empire under a single ruler unified Chinese society.

3 Chinese achievements in technology have had a major effect on the rest of the world.

As you read, keep these ideas in mind. They will help you understand the forces that shaped the development of Chinese civilization and continue to influence China today.

BIG IDEA: RESPECT FOR THE PAST

Confucius based his ideas for reforming society on preserving Chinese traditions.

BIG IDEA: THE RULE OF THE EMPEROR

The first Chinese emperor defeated rival kingdoms to unite China under a single ruler.

BIG IDEA: CHINA AND THE WORLD

Chinese silk reached Europe over a system of trade routes across Central Asia.

此齊小人畫像

CHINESE WRITING

A Gift from the Ancients

From ancient times to today, handwriting as an art form has remained one of China's most respected cultural traditions. Beautiful handwriting takes years to learn and perfect.

A calligrapher at work

A signmaker creates good luck banners for Chinese New Year.

The Chinese character yung, "eternity"

Handwriting as an art is called **calligraphy** (kuh–LIHG–ruh–fee), which in Greek means "beautiful writing." Calligraphers use ink and special brushes to paint Chinese **characters,** the symbols of their ancient writing system. All calligraphers write the same characters, but each artist's brushstrokes are different.

Although there are thousands of different characters in written Chinese, they are all created with a few basic brushstrokes. These include the dot, horizontal and vertical strokes, strokes that slant left and right, and strokes that rise, hook, and turn. All these strokes can be seen in the Chinese character *yung*, meaning "eternity."

To do calligraphy well, the Chinese believe that an artist must blend control with creativity. Good calligraphy reflects qualities such as "bone" (the boldness of a brushstroke) and "blood" (the smoothness of the inking). Many Chinese also believe that calligraphy is good for the spirit. They feel that practicing this art can make a person calmer, healthier, and more content.

Dragon Bones

The earliest known Chinese writing dates back to about 1200 B.C. **Archaeologists,** the scientists who study the remains of peoples and cultures of the past, learned about the origins of Chinese writing in a strange way. Long ago, Chinese doctors gave their patients a medicine they called "dragon bones." Dragon bones were really the bones from cows or turtle shells. Patients ground them into a powder and mixed it in their tea.

In 1899, a man in northern China saw something odd on the dragon bones he had bought. They seemed to be covered with a kind of writing. He was curious about the writing and showed one bone to a historian. This dragon bone eventually led researchers to a nearby city that was once a capital of the ancient Shang dynasty. There, archaeologists dug up hundreds of dragon bones with writing on them.

Oracle bone from the Shang dynasty, around 1500 B.C.

In time, researchers learned how to read the writing. They discovered that the ancient Shang kings had used these bones to try to communicate with gods and learn the future. Such a message from the gods is called an oracle, so the bones are known as **oracle bones.** Priests first scratched a question on an oracle bone, such as, "Will the king have a son?" Then, they heated it, causing the bone to crack. The priests read the answer to the question in the pattern of the cracks.

Later, the correct answer (what actually happened), was added, providing a historical record. The Shang kings stored hundreds of oracle bones at their capital, where archaeologists found them more than 3,000 years later.

The scratches on the oracle bones preserved the earliest form of Chinese writing. They show that, by 1200 B.C., China already had a very complex writing system. The 26 letters of the Roman alphabet that we use represent the sounds of our language. By contrast, each of the hundreds of different characters found on the oracle bones stood for a complete word or idea. Most were **pictographs,** pictures used to represent things. This complex system must have developed over a long period of time. However, archaeologists have not yet found any traces of an earlier form of Chinese writing than that on the dragon bones.

▶ *For more information about the Shang and the Chinese writing system, see page 57.*

WHY IT MATTERS TODAY

China's writing system has had a great influence on Chinese society and culture. Having a written language common to all China's people has helped unify Chinese society. An ancient and honored art form in China, calligraphy is widely practiced today.

ONE SYSTEM FOR ALL

Chinese and English signs hanging side by side in Hong Kong

The modern Chinese writing system has about 50,000 characters. People need to know 2,000 to 4,000 characters just to read a Chinese newspaper. The character system is hard to learn. Most Chinese children learn to read using **pinyin** (pihn–yihn). This is a system for converting Chinese characters into the 26 letters of the Roman alphabet. In 1979, China's government officially ordered the use of pinyin. By the time they are adults, however, most Chinese know how to read and write Chinese characters.

The character system is China's main written language. There is a good reason for this. There are many forms of *spoken* Chinese. They differ from one another as much as French, Italian, and Spanish do. But all of these different forms of spoken Chinese are *written* in the same way. Using the character system, all Chinese can at least read the same symbols and share ideas in writing. The Chinese writing system, a gift from the ancient past, helps unite a huge nation whose people speak many different forms of the Chinese language.

From ancient to modern times, the foundation of Chinese society has always been the family.

Here is an old Chinese tale. Like many Chinese tales, it teaches a lesson.

Min's mother had died when he was very young. His father later remarried and had two more sons. Min's stepmother always dressed her own sons in thick, warm coats, but she gave Min only a thin, lightweight coat. The boy never complained.

One winter day, Min's father discovered the shabby coat his wife had given his oldest son. In a rage, the father ordered his second wife out of the house. But Min begged his father to have mercy on his stepmother. He said, "If she stays, one son will be freezing. But if she leaves, all three sons will suffer from the cold." Hearing this, Min's father changed his mind, and his stepmother became kinder to Min.

FAMILY V

ALUES

CONFUCIUS SAYS:

How to Argue with Mom and Dad

"In serving his parents, a son may argue with them, but gently. When he sees they do not want to follow his advice, he shows even more reverence to them, but should continue to argue. If they punish him, he does not complain."

—Confucius

Respect for Elders

Min's story teaches one of the values of Confucius, the most important thinker in Chinese history. Kongfuzi, or "Master Kung"—*Confucius* is the European form of his name—was born during a violent period in the history of China. He hoped his ideas might help reform Chinese society. His teachings, called **Confucianism,** form a code of social conduct, based on moderation, kindness, and respect for tradition.

Min's story shows what it means to have **"filial piety,"** or respect for one's parents. From ancient times, the Chinese have seen the strength of families as the foundation of their society. Family virtues like filial piety were central to the ideas of Confucius.

In Confucianism, the family was the most important element of society. Confucius believed that families that worked well helped villages work well, which helped kingdoms work well, and so on up to China as a whole. Confucius taught that a family works best when its members understand and carry out their duties and respect one another.

Confucius clearly defined what was expected of each family member. He taught that the most important of all family relationships was the one between a father and his son. (This was because family names were passed down through men.) A father should always treat his son with kindness, and a son should always treat his father with respect.

A quiet scene of Chinese family life in the 1700s

Confucius also described four other basic relationships. These were those between husband and wife, older brother and younger brother, older friend and younger friend, and ruler and subject. In all these relationships, kindness and care were to be responded to with respect.

Confucianism in Daily Life

How did the teachings of Confucius affect everyday life in ancient China? Min's tale shows Confucian family values in action. He is a shining example of filial piety. He respects his stepmother and defends her, even though she is cruel to him. As the oldest son, Min deserves much better treatment than his stepmother's abuse. Min's father is justified in his anger at his wife.

In ancient China, family members played similar roles to the ones in Min's story. The head of the household—the father or sometimes the grandfather—was responsible for providing food and shelter. In return, sons and daughters were expected to show filial piety.

The Chinese honor dead family members at Ching Ming Festival, or "grave-sweeping day."

The teachings of Confucius (right) were based on respect for family relationships.

They had to honor and obey their parents without asking anything. Even adults were required to tell their elderly parents where they were going and whom they would be seeing. The father had the final say about everything that happened in the family.

Filial piety continued long after a parent's death. When the head of a household died, the family mourned for three years. The eldest son became the new head of the family and provided his father with a proper burial. Each household kept a shrine to the family ancestors. Every morning, the eldest son was expected to visit the shrine and inform the ancestors about important family events.

The Chinese valued daughters far less than sons. They had a saying: "Raising daughters is like raising children for another family." This was because, when a girl married, she became a member of her husband's family—and a low-ranking member too. Her only power would be over her own future daughter-in-law, if she were fortunate enough to have one. In a traditional Chinese family, a woman's basic duty was to put others first, herself last.

▶ *For more information about the Chinese family and Confucianism, see pages 56–57 and 59.*

WHY IT MATTERS TODAY

Confucian ideals, such as respect for parents, continue to be very important to the Chinese. In Chinese homes, people build shrines to honor family members who have died. On "grave-sweeping day" in spring, Chinese visit the graves of their ancestors. A family cleans the graves, makes food offerings, and burns "hell money" for the spirits of family members to use in the afterlife.

Lessons for C

> *"A man, though born like a wolf, may, it is feared, become an abnormal weakling. A woman, though born like a mouse, may, it is feared, become a tiger."*
>
> —Chinese saying

The Chinese believed that women were unequal to men, and felt it was natural and proper for men to rule women. Failure to keep up a proper relationship between husband and wife or brother and sister would bring about a breakdown of all the rules of traditional Chinese society.

Women

Most women in China once stayed home. Today, Chinese women leave home to work.

An interesting example of what it meant to be a woman in China under the Han dynasty can be seen in the life and work of Ban Zhao (bahn jow). In most ways, she was a traditional Chinese woman, yet she also became a great historian.

When Ban Zhao was born about A.D. 45, her family did not expect much of her because she was female. Most girls were not educated, but Ban Zhao's mother was, and she taught her daughter to read and write. Ban Zhao had been born into an important family that had long been part of the Chinese emperor's court. Her father was a well-known scholar and court historian. He had begun to write an official history of the first 200 years of the Han dynasty. He died when his daughter was about eight years old, his history still unfinished.

Ban Zhao married at age 14 and went to live with her husband's family, according to Chinese custom. As the lowest ranking member, she "took up the dustpan and the broom," performing household chores as directed by her mother-in-law. Ban Zhao had several children.

From Dust Pans to History

Her husband died young, but she never remarried. A widow usually remained with her husband's family, but Ban Zhao went to the emperor's court and completed her father's unfinished history. In addition, she was appointed to supervise the imperial library. She became a teacher to the leading women of the court and a friend and adviser of the empress. Ban Zhao's history of the Han Empire became a very important work for historians of China. However, she is best known for her book *Lessons for Women,* which she wrote for her daughters.

Ban Zhao felt that she had not brought up her children with sufficient respect for tradition. As a result, she feared that her daughters, "just now at the age for marriage, had not learned the proper customs for married women." So she wrote down some instructions for correct female behavior in everyday life, and asked each of her daughters to write out a copy for herself.

In her book, Ban Zhao mentions three customs that the ancient Chinese observed when a girl was born. First, they placed the baby below the bed, showing that she should always act humbly. Second, they let her play with a bit of broken pottery used as a weight in spinning thread. This meant that she should always work hard. Finally, they announced the baby's birth to her ancestors with an offering. This signified that in her husband's home she should faithfully attend to the worship of the ancestors.

Ban Zhao sums up proper behavior for women by listing four basic ways of acting. A woman should behave modestly, speak only at proper moments, keep herself clean, and be a good homemaker. She tells her daughters that these virtues are easy to possess if a woman "will only treasure them in her heart."

▶ *For more information about the Chinese family and Confucianism, see pages 56–57 and 59.*

WHY IT MATTERS TODAY

In the last 50 years, China has made progress in changing the traditional role of women in Chinese society. In the process, the government has sometimes attacked Confucianism, because of the low status it gives to women. However, Confucian ideas continue to influence Chinese society today, and women in China are still not valued as highly as men.

The First Empe...

"The King of Qin has the heart of a tiger or a wolf. Once he really has his way, he will hold the whole world captive."

—Chinese historian Sima Qian

China is a huge land that was often very difficult to govern. At several times in its history, China split into many warring kingdoms. It often took an extraordinary ruler to restore order and unify the country. China's first emperor, Shi Huangdi, was such a ruler.

Shi Huangdi's capital city had many luxurious palaces.

ror

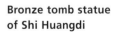

**Bronze tomb statue
of Shi Huangdi**

For more than 180 years, from about 403 to 221 B.C., seven Chinese kingdoms struggled for power. Histories of China call it the Period of Warring States. "The land was divided like a melon," mourned a person who lived during it. One of these warring kingdoms was Qin. Its ruler was named Chao (chow) Cheng.

When he came to the throne at the age of 13, Qin was the most powerful Chinese kingdom. Cheng set out to conquer his six rivals, one by one. Sometimes he used cunning, by sending spies to weaken other governments or by bribing their leaders. When cunning failed to work, he used force. However, the most important thing Cheng did was to keep complete control of each kingdom after he took power. Each conquest became part of his growing empire.

Unifying China

To control his expanding empire, Chao Cheng created a strong central government with tight control over every area of life. In doing this, he followed a set of Chinese ideas called **Legalism.** Legalism completely disagreed with what the Chinese thinker Confucius had taught. Good conduct alone would never improve society.

Shi Huangdi ordered scholars killed and books burned to keep order.

Instead, stern laws and harsh punishments were all-important.

Cheng believed the government should not just maintain order or defeat enemies. It should also shape society, down to the smallest detail. Legalism left a deep mark on Chinese ideas of government. Even today, China's government has strict control over every aspect of Chinese life from politics to the arts to family life.

In his late thirties, Cheng defeated the last enemy kingdom. He gave himself a new name, Shi Huangdi (shee hwahng–dee), "First Emperor." As emperor of all China, he set about to unify his empire. His first step was to create a single system of law and government. He divided the country into 36 districts, each headed by Qin officials. Their loyalty was to him and his central government—not to local interests.

Shi Huangdi worried about rebellion and civil war. He ordered all China's noble families to live in his capital city where he could watch them. He called this policy "strengthening the trunk and weakening the branches." Under Shi Huangdi's eye, these nobles would not be able to build armies to challenge him. Shi Huangdi also took away property from powerful landowners and encouraged poor peasants to work on and manage the farmland.

Shi Huangdi knew that he had to do more than just proclaim that China was one nation. He had to create things that were the same for all Chinese people. The emperor began a program of **standardization** to make Chinese life the same throughout his huge empire. He standardized China's written language and money, so his people could communicate easily and trade with one another. Later, he ordered all weights and measures standardized. Even things like the distance between a pair of wheels on a cart were made uniform, so every vehicle could use China's main roads.

To make travel and trade easier and unify his empire, Shi Huangdi standardized wheel size on carriages.

Many Chinese farms get water from irrigation canals.

Building and Destroying

Finally, Shi Huangdi undertook a huge program of public building. To defend his empire's northern border from invasion, he repaired, strengthened, and linked together existing walls into the barrier known as the Great Wall of China. The emperor built a network of roads linking all parts of China to his capital, Xianyang (syen–yong). He dug irrigation canals to bring water to farms. Some of these canals are still in use today, more than 2,000 years later.

The emperor forced people to work on these projects, and thousands died while working under brutal conditions. This cruelty led to hatred, and Shi Huangdi became the target of several assassination attempts. As he grew older, the emperor became obsessed with a desire to live forever. He invited magicians to his court and made mysterious trips, searching for ways to prolong his life.

Chinese scholars attacked Shi Huangdi both for his cruelty and his study of magic. In response, the emperor had hundreds of scholars put to death. The emperor did not stop there. He ordered most books to be burned, making an exception for those on farming, medicine, and magic.

Shi Huangdi used forced labor for building projects such as his tomb.

All histories except records of Qin were to be destroyed. Shi Huangdi wanted to stop his people from wishing they could follow the old ways.

Suddenly, in 210 B.C., the emperor died while on a journey to find a magic medicine that would make him live forever. Qin rule did not long survive his death. It was not to be "enjoyed by his sons for ten thousand generations," as he had once proclaimed. However, much of Shi Huangdi's work did survive. The nation remained united—in fact, the word *China* comes from the name for the kingdom of Qin.

▶ *For more information about Shi Huangdi, see page 60.*

WHY IT MATTERS TODAY

Shi Huangdi created the first centralized government for all China. Since his time, many Chinese rulers have modeled themselves on him. Like Shi Huangdi, some have ruled with force and have tried to get rid of "old ideas." All these rulers have kept China united as one people and nation to this day.

TOMB WARRIORS

In Pit 1, 38 columns of soldiers stand four abreast, as if marching into battle. Chinese researchers believe that the clay warriors were a re-creation of Shi Huangdi's imperial guard and were meant to accompany him to the next world. In death, the emperor would still be powerful.

Shi Huangdi began work on his tomb soon after he came to power at age 13. Even while the emperor searched for magical potions to make himself immortal, he had more than 700,000 laborers toiling for 36 years to build the huge complex at his capital Xianyang.

In 1974, life-size clay soldiers were found in a pit at the tomb. Since then, researchers have uncovered several more pits at the site. In all, the statues form an army of thousands of foot soldiers, archers, cavalrymen, charioteers, and horses.

To gain insight into ancient techniques and to produce reproductions for sale, a young sculptor copies the head of one of the clay warriors.

Craftsmen molded the soldiers in clay (right), then fired them in ovens at a very high temperature. They used ten different head shapes and finished each statue by hand to make each warrior look different from the next.

The soldiers were originally painted in bright colors. Here (far right), a computer reconstruction shows how the statue of a general would have looked when it came from the hands of Shi Huangdi's craftsmen.

DRIVING ALONG THE GR

One of the measures that Shi Huangdi took to protect his empire was to strengthen the walls defending China's northern border. Added to and restored by other rulers over the centuries, the Great Wall of China still snakes across the Chinese landscape.

EAT WALL

Mr. and Mrs. Wang in front of their home

Walls and People

In ancient times, guards stationed along the wall used smoke signals to warn of invasion. Today, Chinese villagers climb up onto the ruins of an old wall fort to get good cell phone reception. In an old civilization such as China, past and present often interact. Writer Peter Hessler discovered this when he recently drove the entire length of the Great Wall. Hessler traveled 7,436 miles (11,965 km) on his journey. The distance was so great that he divided his trip into two parts—fall and spring. The goal was to reach the far western end of the wall.

In the fall of 2002, he left Beijing, China's current capital city, with a tent, a sleeping bag, and a full tank of gas.

In some places, it is difficult just to find where the Great Wall is. In parts of northeastern China, for example, the wall is now only knee high after years of being torn down and neglected. Hessler tripped over parts that were so low that brush and grass covered them. There are also gaps in the wall. There are even places where the wall is really two or more walls running next to each other.

For Hessler, the people he met were as interesting as the Great Wall itself. He met Mr. and Mrs. Wang, whose village lies next to one section of wall.

...AS THE **GREAT WALL** ITSELF.

Carved out of the Great Wall itself, their home has walls 20 feet (6 meters) thick. "Very warm in the winter, cool in the summer," Mr. Wang told him.

At another spot along the wall, Hessler watched a traveling folk theater troupe perform for a funeral. These performances usually teach a religious lesson or reenact folktales. Wei Fu, the head of the troupe, grinned at Hessler from beneath his make-up. He told Hessler that 80 percent of his business comes from funerals. This funeral for an 80-year-old woman, like others he encountered on his journey, was more a celebration of a life than a display of sorrow.

Q & A:
THE GREAT WALL

Q: **Is the Great Wall a single structure?**

A: The Great Wall is not one structure but many border walls. It would be more accurate to talk about the Great "Walls" of China.

Q: **How old is it?**

A: China's border walls were built at various times during the past 2,200 years. The earliest were begun in the seventh century B.C. and the "newest" parts were not completed until about A.D. 1500.

Q: **How long is it?**

A: The Great Wall constructed by Shi Huangdi was about 1,500 miles (2,400 kilometers) long. The total length of the Great Wall today is over 4,000 miles (6,400 kilometers).

Q: **Can the Great Wall be seen from the moon?**

A: No. This myth was started by Western writers sometime around 1900. However, the wall has been photographed by radar from space.

"Destroy the Hu"

Hessler met a local historian who had an old map of a region of China. All the town names ended in the syllable "hu," an old Chinese name for the **nomads** who lived north of China in what is now Mongolia. The names explained everything about how ancient China saw these neighbors: "Destroy the Hu," "Overawe the Hu," "Slaughter the Hu." When the first sections of the wall were built in the seventh century B.C., Chinese rulers feared invasion from Mongolia. The Great Wall helped unify China against these enemies.

A huge part of the wall's construction began under China's first emperor, Shi Huangdi. He ordered all the older parts of the wall to be joined and

THESE **PERFORMANCES** USUALLY TEACH A **RELIGIOUS LESSON**

A festival parade along the Great Wall

watchtowers built every 200 to 300 yards (180 to 275 meters). Hessler could see some of the ancient watchtowers along his route. The wall itself was formed of cut stone on the outside around a core of stones, dirt, and rubble. Many of the laborers who died building the wall are buried in the core. The wall cost so many lives that it is also called the "Long Graveyard."

OR REENACT FOLKTALES.

Hessler continued driving west into the deserts of northwest China and toward the end of the wall. He passed fewer towns in these last 600 miles (965 kilometers), and even got stopped by the police who wondered what a traveler was doing so far inside China. The last outpost along the wall was high in the mountains. Beyond this point there were no more towns, gas stations, or cars—just open road.

After 25 miles (40 kilometers), Hessler saw a pair of dirt roads branching off the main highway, marked by a sign. From the words on it, he guessed that the two destinations were government run—military installations, perhaps. A left turn led to a place called "Build." A right turn went to "Unite." He took a deep breath and drove straight through.

▶ *For more information about the Great Wall, see page 60.*

WHY IT MATTERS TODAY

The Chinese no longer use the Great Wall to keep people out. On the contrary, the Chinese government is rebuilding parts of it in order to attract tourists to China. For people around the world, the Great Wall remains a powerful symbol of China itself—linking past to present.

Civil service exams in
ancient China

To enrich your family, there is no need to buy good land: Books hold a thousand measures of grain. . . . A young man who wishes to be somebody will devote his time to the Classics. He will face the window and read.

—Chinese emperor Renzong

Joining the Civil Service

Under Han rule, China became a great empire. To govern it, Han rulers needed thousands of government officials. Becoming one of these officials was the path to success in ancient China, but first you had to pass the test.

殿試舉人

Could you devote 20 to 30 years to studying? Could you learn military strategy, civil law, government finance, farming, geography, and poetry? Could you pass an exam that went on for 72 hours? To become a **civil servant,** or government official, in ancient China, you had to pass the **Chinese Imperial Exams.** If you passed, it meant wealth and prestige for you and your family. But it was a tough test.

Tough Test

Studying for the Chinese Imperial Exams and passing them often took almost a lifetime. Only about 2 out of every 100 men who took the tests passed and became civil servants. Some candidates failed the exams many times, but they continued to take them. It was not uncommon for old men to still be taking the exams.

Failing the exam shamed both the candidate and his family. Some tried cheating to pass. The tests were based on knowledge of the works of Confucius. Candidates carried tiny copies of these works that could be hidden in the palm of the hand. One such book was found that contains 68 pages with 80,000 characters, each the size of a pinhead. Some candidates had passages from texts sewn on the insides of their shirts, or written on the inside of the fans they carried.

The system of civil service examinations was created during the Han dynasty. Han rulers realized they needed people of ability and loyalty to help them rule. These civil servants ranged from local governors to the officials who oversaw the emperor's security or handled relations with foreigners.

The civil service exams were based on Confucianism, which stressed the importance of moral conduct and social order. The civil service became an ethical and loyal group who accepted the Confucian teachings.

The earliest exams required the memorization of five Confucian texts. Candidates were later also tested in music, archery and horsemanship, arithmetic, writing, and knowledge of Chinese rituals. By the end of the Han period, the exams had been expanded to include law, taxes, military strategies, and geography. Over time, the examination system was changed. Rulers did not think memorizing was enough. The exams began to stress the understanding of the teachings of Confucianism and the ability to apply that understanding to current problems.

One of China's modern civil servants—a policeman directing traffic in present-day Beijing

Making the Grade

There were generally three to four levels of exams. The exams lasted between 24 and 72 hours. They were given in empty rooms where the candidates were kept isolated. The first level of exams tested the candidates' knowledge of and ability to write poetry. Candidates who did well in these first exams advanced to compete against those from faraway towns.

The next level of exams tested the candidates' memorization of the five Confucian works, as well as other areas of study. Candidates who did well on the second level of tests went on to the national level of tests. This level tested the ability to analyze political problems using their Confucian training.

The system of examinations lasted until 1905, just a few years before the establishment of the Republic of China. At that time, people felt the

exams were outdated and did not properly train officials. The content of the exams may have been outdated, but the idea of choosing civil servants based on their merits was not. The system helped provide well-prepared government workers.

▶ *For more information about the Chinese civil service, see page 61.*

WHY IT MATTERS TODAY

The idea of choosing government officials based on their education and performance remains important. The Chinese civil service examination system has served as a model for many other countries. Today, in China and elsewhere in the world, many government officials are chosen based on merit exams rather than political connections.

The Beauty of

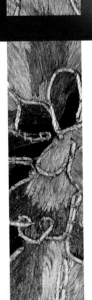

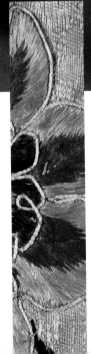

For a long time, only the Chinese knew the secret of making silk. As a result, they were able to establish a highly valuable trade in silk with other peoples of the ancient world.

Silkworms may look harmless enough. They are small, round, slimy, and eat so much that one silkworm will increase its weight 10,000 times in its month-long lifetime. Like other caterpillars, they go through a pupa stage where they live inside self-made cocoons as they transform into moths. Each cocoon is made from a single strand of pure silk. The ancient Chinese learned how to harvest these cocoons, process the silk threads, and weave beautiful cloth from them. First, however, the Chinese had to feed these little worms.

Mothering Silkworms

Silkworms are among the pickiest eaters in the world. For the caterpillars to produce fine silk for cocoons, they have to be fed the right way. Silkworms can eat the leaves of many kinds of trees, but a strict diet of mulberry leaves will make them produce the soft, strong silk that is popular worldwide. The little crawlers eat constantly. Since they breathe through holes on the sides of their bodies, they do not stop eating even to breathe!

The ancient Chinese had strict rules for those who raised silkworms so that the caterpillars could be coaxed into producing high-quality silk. Silkworms were not allowed to hear a dog's bark or any other animal's cry. Bad smells were not allowed in the room with newly hatched caterpillars. The youngest silkworms had to rest on dry mats and had to eat, sleep, and crawl around together. Caterpillars that did not do what most other silkworms were doing were fed to fish.

The young silkworms were sometimes tickled with a chicken feather to encourage their growth. The person who watched over the silkworms had to wear simple clothes so she would not disturb the air too much as she walked. Her job title was "silkworm mother." This tradition of raising silkworms survives today—and with many of the same rules! The women who raise silkworms are not allowed to smoke, wear makeup, or eat garlic.

After the silk cocoons are harvested, artists and weavers create the beauty

Making silk is a long process: The worms (far left) are fed only the best food. The "silkworm mother" (left) cares for the worms. Silk thread is spun from cocoons (above left). Finally, the thread is woven into beautiful fabrics (above right).

of the material. Colorful shirts, flowing skirts, and even high-tech athletic garments are made from silk. Skiers wear silk socks and silk underwear to keep themselves warm and dry. Because of its strength, surgeons can use silk thread to sew up the cuts made during operations.

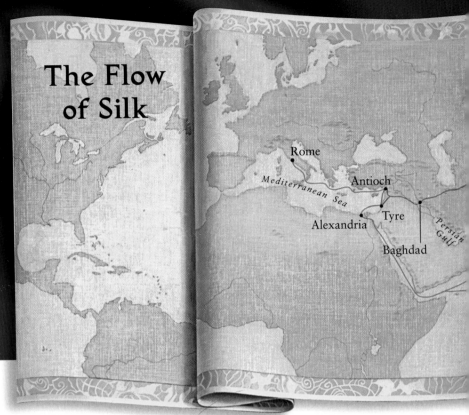

The Flow of Silk

From early in the Han period (map), caravans traveled the Silk Road (red) from China to the Mediterranean. Centuries later, the Silk Road declined when sea routes (blue) proved safer than the long, dangerous land journey.

Past meets present in the Chinese design of this silk robe (far right) inspired by ancient styles.

Rome

Mediterranean Sea

Antioch

Tyre

Alexandria

Baghdad

Persian Gulf

The Silk Road

Like people today, the ancient world loved silk for its beauty, comfort, and strength. Because this fabric is both lightweight and very valuable, silk was an ideal product for ancient traders. As a result, a system of trade routes known as the **Silk Road** developed between China and the countries bordering the Mediterranean Sea.

From the Han capital of Xi'an, the main route cut west through Mongolia. When it reached the harsh Taklimakan Desert, the Silk Road divided into two branches—one northern route and one southern route. After skirting the desert, the two branches rejoined at the city of Kashi in Central Asia. The main route continued westward to the Mediterranean, while other branches turned south to India and the Persian Gulf. No trader traveled the entire length of the Silk Road. Merchants from Europe traded their goods to Central Asian traders who exchanged them with Chinese merchants.

In addition to silk, many other luxury goods passed along these routes. The Chinese also traded furs, tea, perfumes, and chinaware. East Asian traders

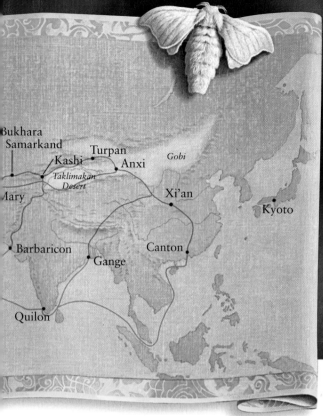

brought spices such as cinnamon, nutmeg, and ginger. Indians traded pepper, pearls, cotton, and ivory. Central Asian peoples sent horses and jade back to China. European merchants traded wool, gold, silver, olive oil, and wine.

For thousands of years, the ancient Chinese controlled the secret of silk-making. But as the fabric spread along the Silk Road—west into Central Asia, then on to Europe—so did the secret of how to produce silk, along with smuggled silkworms. After the secret was revealed, there was no stopping others from creating silk.

▶ *For more information about the Silk Road, see page 62.*

WHY IT MATTERS TODAY

Other things besides trade goods—including ideas and technology—traveled the Silk Road. The Buddhist religion spread from India throughout East Asia along the trade routes. The Chinese invention of paper reached the Islamic world and Europe via the Silk Road. Today's global economy brings peoples from different parts of the world into close contact with each other's cultures.

THE SPIRIT OF
INVENTI

From ancient times, the Chinese have shown a gift for technology. Among China's most significant contributions to world civilization are four great inventions—paper, printing, gunpowder, and the compass.

Fireworks light up the night sky over Tiananmen Square in China's capital city, Beijing.

ON

Woodblocks were coated with paint then pressed on paper to create an image.

What if your textbooks were written on clay tablets? That is what the people of some ancient civilizations used as a writing material. You would need a wheelbarrow instead of a backpack to carry your homework! Paper is one of the basic materials essential in the modern world. And paper was first made in China.

Paper was invented in China around A.D. 105 and quickly came into wide use. The Chinese figured out a way to pound natural ingredients, such as tree bark, bamboo, straw, cotton—even old fishnets—into a pulp. They added water to the pulp and poured a thin layer of the mixture onto a bamboo mat. When they pressed the water out and let the sheet dry, the result was a sturdy, lightweight piece of paper.

Even with paper available, everything still had to be written by hand. It was time-consuming and costly, so only wealthy people were able to own reading materials. Then, the ancient Chinese invented printing, and many copies of a book could be produced in a fairly short time. Their printing process used carved wooden blocks. The Chinese spread ink on the blocks and pressed the blocks onto paper. The pattern of the block now showed up in ink, and the block could be used many times. The Chinese first used printing to print prayers, but the new process eventually allowed them to print whole books.

A tray (above) holds lettering brushes and name stamps for printing. Wheelbarrows (right) made moving heavy items easier.

The invention of paper and printing changed the world, and it certainly changed the way students learn today. If you did need to wheel your heavy books to class, you could still thank the ancient Chinese, since they also invented the wheelbarrow!

Early types of Chinese compass (left)

Chinese celebration with fireworks and kites (right)

More Inventions

The ancient Chinese knew that an iron ore called *lodestone* had magnetic properties. Lodestone attracted metal, and lodestone shavings had the unusual ability to always point to the north. The ancient Chinese learned how to make magnetized iron needles and eventually developed the round magnetic compass.

Long afterward, when the magnetic compass became well known, the invention completely changed travel by sea. Explorers no longer needed to stay close to the coastline or rely on being able to see the position of the sun or stars. Without the fear of becoming lost at sea, they were able to travel great distances. Famous navigators including Christopher Columbus used Chinese-style compasses in their voyages of exploration.

Another Chinese invention that changed the world was gunpowder. The ancient Chinese had discovered, possibly by accident, that they could cause explosions to occur if they mixed the right ingredients together. The Chinese used gunpowder to create colorful fireworks for their celebrations and festivals. Later, in their long struggle against the Mongols, they developed weapons, such as the cannon, that forever changed the way wars were fought.

▶ *For more information about Han technology, see page 62.*

WHY IT MATTERS TODAY

As Chinese inventions spread throughout the world, they had major effects on history. The use of gunpowder, for example, made modern wars much more destructive.

Ancient China

This Overview provides a brief summary of the most important people, places, and events of ancient China. Its purpose is to help you better understand the historical background of the articles in this book.

River Valley Settlements

Like most early civilizations, early Chinese cultures developed in river valleys. People were drawn to the fertile soil and plentiful water supplies in the river valley of the Huang He, or Yellow River. Deserts and mountains that separated China from the rest of Asia helped protect this river valley civilization from invasion.

By about 5000 B.C., the early Chinese lived together in permanent settlements.

They learned to survive floods, dust storms, and extremes of heat and cold. They grew millet for grain and hemp to make into clothing. They raised pigs and sheep, made polished stone tools, and built permanent shelters.

The Chinese Family

Early Chinese homes were built in clusters. Some historians believe that people lived in family or clan groups. This would be the earliest evidence of a tradition that continues even today in Chinese culture. As civilization grew, powerful families assumed leadership. They established dynasties in which the right to rule was passed from father to son.

Major Events

1200 B.C.
Earliest Chinese writing

2000 B.C.

1000 B.C.

1600 B.C.
Shang dynasty founded

551 B.C.
Confucius born

The Chinese family unit was highly organized. When a woman married, she became part of her husband's family. With the exception of her parents and grandparents, her husband's ancestors became her ancestors. Typically, the newly married couple lived with the husband's parents. The oldest male in the family was the head of the household. Everyone in the family contributed what they owned for the benefit of all. The Chinese believed that family members continued to help the family even after their death. Family duties included supporting their ancestors by "feeding" them with respect and worship.

Shang bronze vessels and the molds used to make them

The Shang Dynasty

The Shang dynasty is the first for which historical evidence has been found. Sometime about 1600 B.C., a people known as the Shang took control of the Huang He civilizations in northern China. They created and controlled a loose group of city-states, each made up of a city and its surrounding settlements. These city-states were ruled by the king and nobles who lived inside the city walls. Peasants lived outside the walls and farmed the land, giving a portion of their harvest to the nobles. The Shang developed a system of writing largely based on pictographs. The Shang created the first Chinese calendar, and were experts in working bronze into weapons, as well as beautiful vessels and sculptures. Shang kings prayed to the gods of wind, earth, clouds, sun, and moon for good crops and other blessings. They also prayed to their ancestral spirits to plead with the most powerful of the Shang gods, Shang-ti, or "the lord on high," who ruled over the lesser gods.

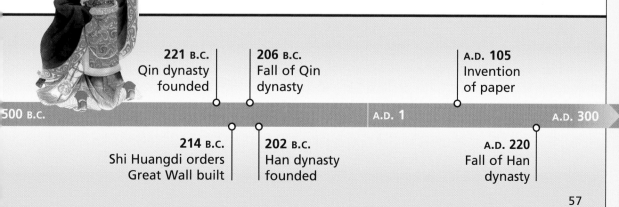

221 B.C.
Qin dynasty founded

206 B.C.
Fall of Qin dynasty

A.D. 105
Invention of paper

500 B.C.

A.D. 1

A.D. 300

214 B.C.
Shi Huangdi orders Great Wall built

202 B.C.
Han dynasty founded

A.D. 220
Fall of Han dynasty

The Zhou Dynasty

The Mandate of Heaven

The last of the Shang kings was corrupt. The Chinese people would not accept this, even in their rulers. About 1027 B.C., the Zhou, a people from the west, formed alliances with other tribes. They invaded and conquered the Shang kingdom. The new Zhou king told the people that Heaven appoints the king to see to their welfare. This is the "order" or "mandate" of Heaven. If the king fails to take care of the people, Heaven gives the mandate or power to another—in this case, the Zhou.

Feudal Rule

The Zhou started a practice known as feudalism. The king appointed kinsmen from his own and other loyal noble families as rulers of more than 200 city-states. The noblemen built armies of men from high-ranking families. The peasants worked the land in return for food and protection. By the 800s, the powerful feudal lords had grown less loyal to the king.

In 771 B.C., raiders from the north invaded western Zhou. The king was killed and his son fled to the Eastern Zhou capital, but the dynasty had been seriously weakened.

Zhou Technology and Trade

Farmers made many advances in agriculture. They began to grow rice and wheat in addition to millet. They learned to rotate their crops and to use fertilizer. The demand for luxury items increased. Wealthy people owned objects of bronze, gold, silver inlays, lacquerware, and silk. Bronze coins have been found in large trading centers. And the people turned their knowledge of working bronze to working iron for weapons and tools.

The Period of Warring States

After the fall of western Zhou, feudal lords continued to battle. Some tried diplomacy to settle their differences. They held conferences, signed treaties, and made alliances. But strong lords continued to conquer weaker ones. In 403 B.C., all attempts to reach agreement ended, and the Period of Warring States began. By the fourth century B.C., only seven or eight large kingdoms remained. Armies grew, as did a professional government nobility who called themselves "superior men." During the Period of Warring States, China moved closer and closer to becoming a single kingdom under a powerful leader.

This brass belt buckle shows the feuding states.

Symbol of yin and yang

Chinese Philosophy—Yin and Yang

The Period of Warring States led many Chinese thinkers to seek ways to restore harmony to their people. Ancient Chinese tradition said that harmony required a balance of opposing forces, which they called *yin* and *yang*. For example, a balance between rain and drought produced good crops. If the forces were out of balance, people suffered.

Confucianism

Confucius was a leading Chinese thinker. He believed that peace would come back when China returned to its traditional values. People must know their proper place in society and perform the duties of that position. Confucius stressed the virtue of *jen*, kindness, concern for others. When asked if there was one rule to practice for all one's life, Confucius said,

"What you do not want done to yourself, do not do to others." We now call this idea the Golden Rule. According to Confucius, even rulers must show *jen*. "When a prince's personal conduct is correct, his government is effective without the issuing of orders. If his personal conduct is not correct, he may issue orders, but they will not be followed."

Daoist priests

Daoism

Dao means "the way." Daoism (DOW–izm) teaches that the universe and nature have an underlying pattern. The goal of man should be to fit into that pattern. The pattern cannot be described, it just has to be lived. "He who knows does not speak; he who speaks does not know." The goal of Daoism is to bring Heaven, Earth, and man into harmony. To follow the Dao, a person must forget about rules and knowledge. He must act with simplicity and humility, and turn to nature for peace and harmony. Daosim greatly influenced Chinese art, which often shows ideal landscapes.

Legalism

Legalists said that strictly enforced laws, rather than the personal balance urged by Confucianism and Daoism would restore the peace. Legalists believed that people were naturally selfish and could not be trusted. "Men have likes and dislikes. Thus they can be controlled by rewards and punishment. Force keeps the people under control." Legalists believed that the king should rule by force. The next ruling dynasty of China would use Legalism to create a unified empire of China.

China's First Empires

The First Emperor—Shi Huangdi

After nearly 900 years, the Zhou dynasty ended. The Qin, the strongest of the seven surviving states, defeated other Chinese kingdoms and took control of China in 221 B.C. The first Qin ruler took the name Shi Huangdi, which means "First Emperor." The Qin empire lasted only 15 years, but left behind two important contributions. It brought the city-state kingdoms into a single unified empire that continued for more than 2,000 years. And the name of the empire, China, came from the name of the dynasty.

Shi Huangdi replaced the old feudal system by dividing the country into provinces and counties. He appointed governors and judges to rule these regions. But many, particularly the well-educated, disliked the emperor's harsh Legalism. He forbade them to discuss his policies.

If they did, he had them executed or sent into exile. The emperor ordered that all books on Confucianism and Daoism be burned. The only books he spared were on technical subjects, such as farming or medicine. A famous Chinese historian said that Shi Huangdi "killed men as though he could never finish, he punished men as though he was afraid he would never get around to them all."

The Great Wall

The emperor was also obsessed with protecting his territory from nomadic people from the north. During earlier dynasties, kingdoms had built walls to protect their borders. The emperor ordered that these walls be joined.

The Ten Thousand Li (a unit of measurement) Wall, as it is known in China, was 1,500 miles (2,400 kilometers) long, from 15 to 50 feet (5 to 15 meters) high, and from 15 to 25 feet (5 to 8 meters) wide. The emperor's fear extended beyond his death in 210 B.C. When his tomb was discovered in the 1970s, 6,000 life-size clay soldiers and horses stood guard.

The Han

Several years after the death of the Qin emperor, a peasant general named Liu Bang assumed the title of emperor. He reminded the people of the Mandate of Heaven. Heaven, he said, had given him the divine authority to rule because the previous emperor had not taken care of the people. Liu Bang kept the governmental structure begun by the Qin. However, he was heavily influenced by Confucianism and wished to restore the yin and yang of government. He lifted the ban on books and invited scholars to advise him.

The Great Wall

A Han emperor welcomes a scholar.

The Civil Service

At the beginning of the Han dynasty, China was the largest country in the world and had more than 60 million people. Governing such a huge empire required a bureaucracy, a system where different parts of government have specialized duties. The Han emperors tried different forms of organization. They kept those that worked and changed those that did not until they had an efficient bureaucracy.

The strongest Han emperor, Wudi, began the civil service. Family influence still counted in getting a government job, but men had to prove their worth by taking an examination. Those who sought the highest offices studied for their tests at the imperial university. They read the works of Confucius, which the emperor believed held the key to good government. Many scholars became government officials, known as mandarins.

Although anyone could take the exams, boys from the peasant class rarely had enough money to pay for the studies.

Expansion of the Han Empire

With an efficient bureaucracy to manage the empire, Wudi pushed its borders even farther. His armies marched north into what is now Korea and south into present-day Vietnam. The nomads who lived on the steppes to the northwest were more of a problem. Wudi used diplomacy, bribes, and military force, eventually conquering the tribes south of the Gobi. Other nomadic leaders soon learned that if they pretended to accept the emperor's rule, he would reward them with great riches. But to maintain this huge empire, Han emperors heavily taxed the people. Eventually, this would lead to unrest and revolt.

The Decline of the Han

Despite the growth of the empire, and the prosperity that came to scholars and traders, the lives of the peasants changed little. They struggled to even raise enough food to survive. But the government demanded that they contribute both taxes and personal labor. Each year, they had to leave their farms to work on roads, canals, and other government projects. In addition to peasant rebellions, other power struggles weakened the empire. One general after another came to power, acting as dictators. By A.D. 220, four centuries of Han rule came to an end.

Legacy of Ancient China

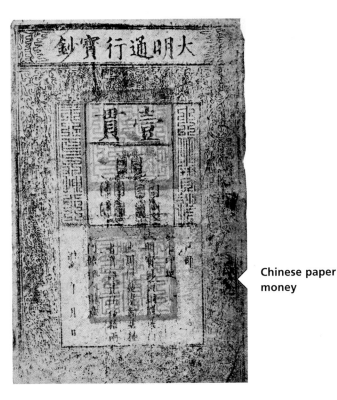

Chinese paper money

Han Technology and Trade

During the Han Empire, Chinese astronomers calculated the length of the year, invented sundials and water clocks, and divided the day into 12 equal periods. In mathematics, the Chinese were the first to use place values in numbers. They invented wheelbarrows and the compass. In A.D. 105, an official in the imperial court ground together the inner bark of a mulberry tree, bamboo fibers, and water. He poured this mixture onto a flat piece of coarsely woven cloth and let the water drain through. The fibers remaining on the cloth dried, forming a writing material that was lightweight and easy to produce—paper.

The Silk Road

Silk had been known in China since about 2500 B.C. Because of the difficulty in making it, silk was used mainly by royalty. During the Han dynasty, silk became a form of payment. Farmers paid their taxes in grain and silk. Civil servants were paid in silk. Prices of goods were calculated in lengths of silk. The Chinese carefully guarded the secret of silkmaking. Smuggling silkworms or their eggs out of the country was punishable by death. Because of its rarity, silk became highly prized in trade with other countries. Silk was carried to the west in caravans along a 9,000-mile trail called the Silk Road. Soon, there was growing trade in other Chinese luxuries, such as exotic furs, spices, lacquer and precious stones.

Silk robes

GLOSSARY

archaeologist a scientist who studies the remains of peoples and cultures of the past

calligraphy handwriting as an art form

characters the symbols of a writing system

Chinese Imperial Exams the examination system used to select civil servants in China from the Han dynasty until 1905

civil servant a government official

civil service government department that hires workers to fill other government jobs

Confucianism the teachings of the Chinese thinker Confucius

dynasty a ruling family; also the period during which it is in power

filial piety respect for parents, a central ideal of Confucianism

Legalism the Chinese idea of government that people can only be controlled by stern laws and harsh punishments

nomads people who move from place to place, seeking food, water, and grazing land for their animals

oracle bones ancient animal bones and tortoise shells that preserve the earliest known form of Chinese writing

pictograph a picture used to represent a thing

pinyin the system for changing Chinese characters into the letters of the Roman alphabet, which was officially adopted by the Chinese government in 1979

Silk Road the system of trade routes across Central Asia, along which merchants carried silk and other luxury goods between China and the West

silt the fertile layer of mud and sand left by a flooding river

standardization making things the same, such as creating one language and one system of measurement

INDEX

Chinese artists made many images of the camels that carried most of the goods that traveled along the Silk Road.